PRACTICAL PARENTING AND LEARNING DISABILITIES

Wrinkles in Teaching: A Series of Guidebooks for Teachers

Wrinkle is "a useful piece of information," and one dictionary illustrates, "Learning the *wrinkles* from someone more experienced saves time." In the case of teaching, it also promotes faster, more effective student learning, it prevents unnecessary and frustrating bouts of trial and error, and it results in greater satisfaction with the work. The "someone more experienced" is Billie Birnie, who taught successfully in elementary, middle, and senior high schools and then went on to observe and teach hundreds of teachers and, eventually, to write about her observations and experiences. Her books, designed for both elementary and secondary teachers, are short, practical, and down-to-earth conversations about the craft of teaching. *Successful Classroom Management and Differentiated Instruction* is the first in the series. Other topics to come:

- *Organizational Strategies for Thinking and Writing*
- *Cooperative Learning*
- *Critical Thinking*
- *Assessing Writing Skill*

Readers are welcome to suggest additional topics for the series.

Titles in the series:

Practical Parenting and Learning Disabilities: A Simple Guide for Teachers and Parents, by Susan Maynard

PRACTICAL PARENTING AND LEARNING DISABILITIES

A Simple Guide for Teachers and Parents

Susan Maynard

ROWMAN & LITTLEFIELD
Lanham • Boulder • New York • Toronto • Plymouth, UK

Published by Rowman & Littlefield
4501 Forbes Boulevard, Suite 200, Lanham, Maryland 20706
www.rowman.com

10 Thornbury Road, Plymouth PL6 7PP, United Kingdom

British Library Cataloguing in Publication Information Available

Library of Congress Cataloging-in-Publication Data Available

ISBN 978-1-4758-1044-8 (pbk. : alk. paper) — ISBN 978-1-4758-1045-5 (electronic)

∞™ The paper used in this publication meets the minimum requirements of American National Standard for Information Sciences—Permanence of Paper for Printed Library Materials, ANSI/NISO Z39.48-1992.

Printed in the United States of America

CONTENTS

ACKNOWLEDGMENTS ix

PART 1: PRACTICAL PARENTING 1

1 Early Childhood Issues 3

Playpens 3
Carrying and Pushing Children in Strollers 4
Toilet Training 6
Crying Isn't All Bad 7
Babying Children 8

2 As Children Grow 9

Bedtimes 9
Mealtimes 12
No! 14
Privilege and Entitlement 14
Limits and Rules 15
Admitting You Made a Mistake 16
Chores 16
General Responsibility 18

3 A Word about Teens 21

4	Random Thoughts on Parenting Children of All Ages	23
	Friends	23
	Cell Phones and All Electronic Devices	24
	TV, Computers, Video Games, Facebook, Tweeting, and the Like	24
	Schedules	26
	Homework	27
	Other School Issucs	28
	Parents Need Time for Themselves	29
	Discipline	30
	Notes	31
PART 1:	**SUMMARY: COMMON SENSE**	33
PART 2:	**LEARNING DISABILITIES**	35
5	How Do You Recognize Learning Disabilities?	39
	At School	39
	At School and at Home	40
6	Types of Learning Interferences	41
	Auditory Interferences (The Inability to Process or Understand What One Hears)	41
	Visual Perception and Visual/Motor Interferences	42
	Dyslexia—Difficulty with Reading or Interpreting the Written Word	42
	Motor/Spatial-Directionality Interferences	43
	Attention Interferences	43
	Speech and Language Interferences	44
	Emotional Interferences	45
7	What Tests Assess Learning Interferences?	47
	Tests for Auditory Interferences	47
	Tests for Motor or Spatial Interferences	48
	Tests for Attention Deficit	48
	Tests for Emotional Interferences	48

8 Suggested Strategies for Teachers 51

9 Suggested Strategies for Parents 59

10 What If Your Child's School Professionals or Pediatrician Recommends a Psycho-Educational Battery of Testing? 65

PART 2: SUMMARY 67

Other Resources 68

Websites 69

ABOUT THE AUTHOR 71

ACKNOWLEDGMENTS

I would like to take this opportunity to thank five friends and colleagues for their support and encouragement that made this second-edition booklet possible: Billy Birnie, Ph.D.; Marie Hero; Penelope Arango; Marilyn Rawlings; and Marse Dare. I would also like to acknowledge my husband, Carl, for his help, time, and patience.

PART I

PRACTICAL PARENTING

After I created the first booklet, I find that I have not changed my mind about parenting skills but would emphasize what I said previously: "It appears to me that parenting has become a more difficult task than it used to be. Now, a few years later, I believe that the electronic devices that children have or could obtain have made it even more complicated. That being said, I believe that parenting has some very basic concepts that still hold true today."

I have seen more anxious young children in my office than in years past. Although there may be other reasons, many of today's children have few, if any, limits or guidelines about what they are allowed or not allowed to do. This makes them anxious and fearful because no one seems to be in control of various situations. Young children thrive on having routines, understanding what is expected of them, and knowing that someone is in charge.

It appears to me that some parents are afraid to discipline their children. They worry that saying "no" may damage their small child's ego. "Running the show" is a huge burden for children. It may make them feel insecure and even overwhelmed. Some children become obsessive in their mannerisms if they have no limits.

In all my years as a psychologist, I have observed that the sooner children learn the rules of life (reasonable ones), the happier and more secure they feel. This pamphlet addresses these rules and the specific times when they can and should be applied.

PART 1

These thoughts and suggestions are not offered as criticism of a particular parenting style. They are simply a guide that may make life with your children easier and more enjoyable. The ideas are straightforward and simply stated in an easy-to-carry, handy booklet. There are specific suggestions and comments about everyday living with your children. The goal is to have contented, courteous, confident children who are conscientious and demonstrate good character.

1

EARLY CHILDHOOD ISSUES

PLAYPENS

In the beginning there were playpens, those funny-looking mesh or wooden containers that held children. Suddenly playpens were considered to be "out," possibly because the word *pen* connoted restriction and/or punishment. Playpens are now referred to as "pack-and-plays." Some suggest they would restrict children's movements and therefore constrict their inventiveness and creativity. I believe this is not true. However, I feel the exact opposite is true:

1. A child in a pack-and-play may safely and comfortably sit, stand, or climb. A child in a pack-and-play may nap, play with toys, or eat. He may choose between Cheerios or raisins placed in the pack-and-play. All these decisions are up to the child!

2. If there is no pack-and-play, a child can wander at will around many rooms. A parent or a caregiver must focus solely on the child to keep him from putting his fingers in electric sockets or climbing and jumping from high places. You get the idea. The child is constantly being observed and is the center of attention. This is not good for either the child or the adults who must give up their own activities to watch him.

3. Even daily tasks, such as washing dishes, folding laundry, or vacuuming, must be postponed until children are napping or asleep for the night. This leaves little time for adults to pursue their interests and enjoy conversation and interactions. This makes life, as well as parenting, much more difficult than is necessary or desirable.

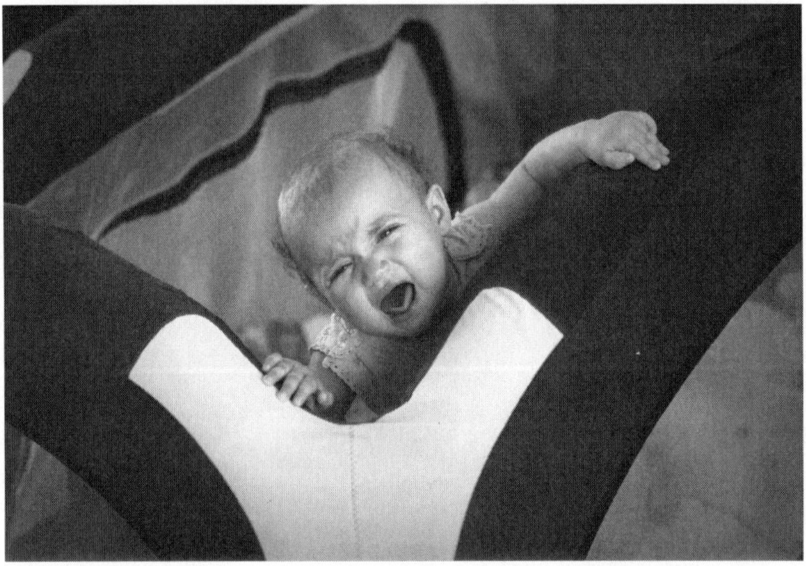

CARRYING AND PUSHING CHILDREN IN STROLLERS

Long after babyhood, children are being carried or pushed in strollers when they should be practicing their walking and running. Some of the children I have seen in strollers are big enough to be pushing a baby in the stroller! Instead, their long legs are tucked up underneath them, and they are riding.

1. Is this because everyone is in such a hurry that we don't have time for a two-year-old to toddle along?

2. Carrying children and transporting them in strollers sends them the message that they are all-important and everyone should cater to them. Instead of being just one part of the family, they are at the center of attention. Parents

need to be at the center because they are the most important part of the family. Understanding this concept is important for a well-balanced family life and gives a child a sense of security and comfort.

3. Carrying heavy toddlers is not good for young and slightly older backs. It deprives youngsters of the exercise that benefits them and delays the process of their growing as individuals who are able to walk by themselves.

TOILET TRAINING

1. This is a messy subject in more ways than one. The basic premise here is that it is the parents' decision when this momentous task should be begun and accomplished. It is not up to the child to decide.

2. Parents should watch for signs of readiness and suggest that using the "potty" would be a "nice" idea. This might begin about the age of two. Bear in mind that some children are easier to deal with than others.

3. One doesn't need to be harsh or demanding, just firmly suggestive.

4. Children need to be informed quietly and firmly: "Everyone uses the toilet or potty, so you need to also."

5. It takes time—lots of it—and consistency. Placing the child on his small toilet and suggesting cheerfully that he should "go" must be done frequently during the day.

6. A small prize or token of your appreciation is a positive idea to reward his success. (I've always believed that a little bribery goes a long way when raising children.)

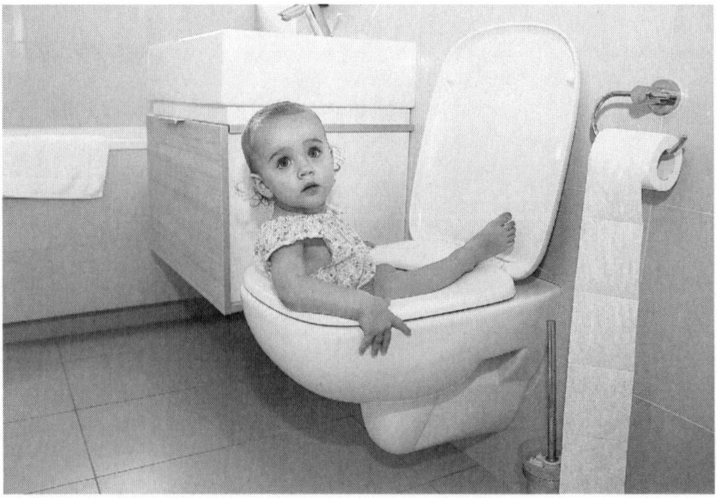

7. Praise is also positive and beneficial for many children. If potty training is your major goal and you are determined, you can accomplish this within two weeks, although some children may take a little longer.

8. Don't give up or give in. Don't lose your temper or good humor. Using the potty is a natural habit, and it will happen eventually, to everyone's delight and benefit.

CRYING ISN'T ALL BAD

1. In the past it was said that crying babies were exercising their lungs. I am not sure this is true, but I do feel that babies and children need to cry, and the release is good for them. Why do we have tears in the first place? Nowadays it seems that children should not have to cry, or they should be immediately soothed, cheered, and picked up when they cry.

2. On the one hand, children should learn that adults can't be manipulated by their tears and tantrums.

3. On the other hand, it is important to determine if a physical problem is causing a child to cry excessively.

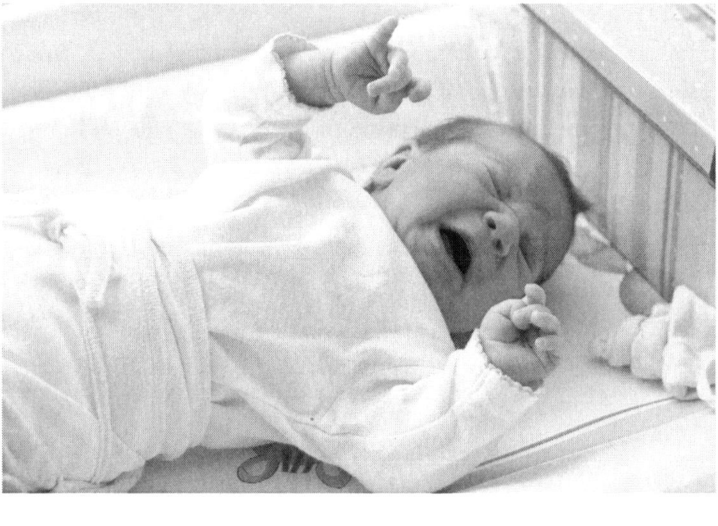

CHAPTER 1

BABYING CHILDREN

1. Babying children for too long sometimes is a cultural matter. This practice certainly affects children and promotes immature behavior. If a child is treated like a baby, he or she certainly will act like one.

2. Healthy development depends on a child growing out of certain necessities of infancy, such as drinking from a bottle and sleeping in his parents' room or perhaps even in their bed.

3. Children respond to being treated as maturing, developing individuals when they begin to learn appropriate skills, such as drinking from a cup, using the toilet, walking on their own, and sleeping in their own beds. I have known parents and grandparents who still give their four-year-olds bottles when they go to bed. This makes the very direct statement to the child: "You are still my baby!"

4. Sometimes these same parents will demand responsibility in other areas. When the child has not had to be responsible for anything else, this is very confusing. It is hard to be a baby in some areas and a responsible human being in others.

5. Nannies and grandparents who are caregivers for children when both parents are not at home may be particularly susceptible to wanting a child to remain a baby. Nannies wish to be loved by their young charges. Sometimes it is easier just to do various tasks rather than asking a youngster to do them. Then the child cannot accuse the nanny of being mean when his parents return home. Nannies want to hold onto their jobs, so they may be too lenient with the children. Grandparents have a vested interest in having their grandchildren remain young. It makes them feel young to have babies around.

2

AS CHILDREN GROW

BEDTIMES

1. Establishing a regular, specific bedtime is very important for all children. Bedtime routines give children a sense of order and security, as well as adequate sleep.

2. Most young children need ten to twelve hours of sleep. As they reach the teen years, usually eight to ten hours will suffice. When children do not get enough sleep, they become crabby and whiny or even listless and unmotivated.

3. Regardless of how much sleep a child has had, he or she must go to school, participate in extracurricular activities, and do homework. How can children be successful when they are always tired? I suspect that there are some unfortunate children who never experience the feeling of being well rested and eager to start a new day.

4. Staying up late on weekends disturbs a child's sleep cycle and makes his regular routine harder to manage. Maintaining consistency in a child's schedule works best for everyone in the family. Of course there are occasional exceptions when Great Uncle Harry is visiting or a special event takes place.

5. It seems particularly difficult for some children to stay in bed or go to sleep. Parents must insist that their children stay in bed. Sometimes soft music will help a child fall asleep. Television does not encourage sleep, but reading to him- or herself may be beneficial.

6. If the child is young, his or her parents may agree to read one story every night. However, if the hour becomes late due to procrastination or fooling around, the parents must say, "We have to skip your story tonight so you will have adequate time to sleep." If the problem continues, other appropriate consequences can be applied, such as having to go to bed fifteen minutes earlier the next night.

7. If your child gets up and comes to you after being put to bed, take him or her calmly back to bed. If this happens more than once, don't give up or give in. Be firm and close his or her door if you have to. It may take some doing if this is a habit, but you must persevere. Otherwise the unwanted behavior will continue, and your child will disturb you every evening.

8. Sleep deprivers:

1. Children seem to be doing many activities after school. Some children I've known are doing four or five different activities at the same time: dance, piano, soccer, cheerleading, swimming, and so on.

   These children do not have time to do everything required of them in a day, such as homework or having family meals together. They are also getting too few hours of sleep just to keep up. Here is where the word *no* comes into play. (This word is discussed more fully later.) A child must be asked to choose a reasonable amount of activities, and you, the parent, can say "no."
2. Another real interference with bedtime is what seems to me as an excessive amount of "homework" from school. Many children have three or more hours of add-on work (homework) after their school day is officially done. I have seen and heard all too frequently that kindergarteners have homework. I find this to be ridiculous and unacceptable.

   There are no studies that I know of that prove that more is better in the case of homework. This makes good sense to me. Homework should serve the teacher with proof that what he or she has taught was learned. Too much homework and too many activities = too little time for rest, sleep, and relaxation.

MEALTIMES

1. Mealtimes should be scheduled as consistently as possible. Children need food at specific times each day.

2. Meals should provide a peaceful time for the family to catch up on everyone's activities and news of the day. Various topics can be discussed calmly, and family members can enjoy one another's company.

3. Food should not be the major focus of conversation at a meal. There is no need for a child to finish everything on his plate. A child might be required to try everything that is served by taking just a bite. If he does not care for the food, there should be no further discussion. In general, there should be no substitutions that are different from the rest of the family's meal.

4. Little children do not always know what they wish to eat, as they have had too few experiences. Therefore, as a general rule, they should not be given choices. It is a burden for toddlers to have too many choices and they simply become confused. This may lead to eating problems later on.

5. The television set and cell phones should be turned off during a meal. Time together without interruption should be the priority. This is the one opportunity during the day when families and invited guests have time to learn about one another's activities and plans. Everyone needs this break in the day's routine.

6. Children who are unruly or disruptive during a meal should be sent from the table so the rest of the family can eat in peace. The misbehaving child can go to his room or have a time out. Being sent from the table could mean missing the meal. No one has ever starved by skipping one meal. However, this consequence will demonstrate clearly to your child that the priority at mealtime is to have a pleasant and relaxing time together.

NO!

1. What is wrong with the word *no*? It is straightforward, to the point, and does not require an explanation most of the time.

2. Children who don't understand that the word *no* really means no may actually be put in physical danger. If the child is near a fire or a busy street, he must respond to adult commands immediately. Taking time for lengthy explanations may endanger the child's life.

3. Children do not need explanations for all their parents' decisions or rules. In fact, it is sometimes confusing or annoying to have too much discussion about a particular command or request. Children as young as two years of age frequently know when something is wrong or off limits. They do not need lengthy explanations about why they are being sent to their rooms or going in time out. They understand! As children grow older, they find debriefings annoying and boring. Lecturing may bring on more undesirable behavior.

4. I have watched mothers bargaining with their children in stores of all kinds. Instead of saying "no" and just leaving, they spend time making excuses: "No, honey, we don't have time" or "That is not good for you" and so on. Equivocation only leads to arguments and temper tantrums or tears.

5. Children are more comfortable and secure when they know the limits and the rules of their homes. There should not be too many rules, but the really important areas should include: bedtime, mealtime, and general acceptable behavior and good manners. The word *no* helps to define clearly these rules and limits.

PRIVILEGE AND ENTITLEMENT

1. Children who have no routines or rules to follow may begin to feel that they are privileged characters. They believe that the world revolves around them. They are therefore entitled to endless attention and should be the recipients of everyone's indulgence.

2. This is not the way the world works. Imagine a preschool teacher having fifteen privileged and entitled toddlers to deal with. School sometimes provides the first experience when a child has to do what he or she is told. A child may be baffled by these new commands that the teacher assumes he or she knows and will follow. When the child refuses, a certain amount of chaos results.

3. Children raised without rules feel they are more important than other people, including their parents. This concept is reinforced every day as their parents give into their whims, let them stay up to all hours, and allow them to watch endless TV.

4. Children are sometimes permitted to attend adult activities and pastimes where they are again made to feel that they are much too important. I have seen the "adorable" two-year-old running from table to table in a fine restaurant. He becomes less adorable as you are trying to have a peaceful evening and a nice meal without interruption.

5. There are few parties these days in which children are not included. They again become the center of attraction and must be supervised closely so they will not get into trouble. Therefore, there is little adult conversation about adult topics and no time to be free of worry about the little ones charging around at record speeds.

LIMITS AND RULES

1. Children thrive when they know what is going to happen and what is expected of them. Routines and knowing the limits provide comfort, security, and love to children of all ages.

2. Bedtimes, mealtimes, and other routine events should be scheduled as often as possible at definite times so children know what to expect. Older children then can plan their extracurricular activities and agendas around the family's routine whenever possible.

3. I remember telling my teenage daughter, who was involved in many activities at school and outside our home, that she was expected to be home for dinner at least three nights a week. The specific nights were flexible as her schedule changed. We were able to accomplish this so it suited everyone in the family. It provided time for catching up, pleasant conversations, and planning for the future.

4. Children become anxious and insecure when basic rules and routines are not established or adhered to.

5. There should be as few basic rules as possible, and their infractions should be dealt with as quickly and consistently as possible. Consistency is one of the cornerstones of successful parenting. It is also one of the most difficult to maintain. Say what you mean, and mean what you say. Stick to your decisions, and don't back down except on rare occasions (for example, if your child is ill).

6. The consequences for misbehavior should be appropriate and related to the problem if possible. Children need to understand this lesson of life. All actions have consequences.

ADMITTING YOU MADE A MISTAKE

1. Don't be afraid to say you are sorry when you make a mistake. Admitting you have made a mistake and apologizing for it make a very positive impression on children.

2. Children will be demonstrably happier if you are able to admit that sometimes you are wrong.

CHORES

1. In general, people feel good about themselves when they accomplish things. This includes children, so it is important for them to have chores.

2. Chores don't have to make Cinderellas of one's children. However, it is nice for a child to hear that he did a good job of making his bed or setting the table.

3. Allowances should not be attached to chores. Chores are done because children are part of a family and everyone is expected to contribute to the family in some way.

4. Allowances should be given so children will learn about money and its value. Children enjoy having their own money to spend as they wish and learn the value of it.

GENERAL RESPONSIBILITY

1. Children need to learn responsibility early. Toddlers as young as two can pick up their toys with your help.

2. Five-year-olds can put their dirty clothes in the hamper and even make their beds. Don't be a perfectionist. Strive for general compliance.

3. When children accomplish something and are told "good job," they feel pleased with themselves. Mastering various tasks gives people of all ages feelings of confidence and self-esteem.

4. Doing small chores at home, such as clearing his place at the table, taking out the trash, or feeding the dog, makes a child feel capable and that he is contributing to the family unit.

5. These family responsibilities carry over into more sophisticated tasks, such as doing one's homework.

Having said "children should do their homework," there has reached a point now when homework is excessive. What can you do to help your child

keep his or her responsibility intact? Acknowledge that you think it is too much homework to your child. Empathize with him or her. Try to maintain bedtimes. Finally go talk to his or her teacher. If this is an unsuccessful task, go to see the principal and the superintendent. (I am not kidding.) It is very important.

If this becomes troublesome, you should solicit some allies. Line up as many other parents who feel the same way, and go visit the previously mentioned people. This is important for your child's well-being. I have seen too many stressed, anxious, and depressed children because they are under so much pressure, a lot stemming from too much homework!

6. I have been from time to time amazed to hear parents state, "His only responsibility is his homework! Why isn't he responsible?" A child doesn't know how to be responsible for something like homework if he has not had such previous responsibilities as simple chores.

3

A WORD ABOUT TEENS

Most of the aforementioned ideas also apply; however, there are a few basic premises to note about teenagers.

1. Teens need to be busy. Never was the statement "Idle hands are the devil's playmate" so relevant. Not all children are athletes; however, athletics are one of the best ways to keep children out of trouble. Some children are more interested in individual sports rather than team sports. Every child

needs an activity that he is involved in, such as band, drama club, and so on, that provides enjoyment as well as a social life. Children who are busy don't have time to get involved with drugs or alcohol or spend too much time on electronic devices.

3. It is naïve to think that most children, even yours, are not going to try these time wasters and fillers. If teenagers participate in a sport, they will have to focus on keeping their bodies in shape to perform well. This may prevent abuse of drugs and alcohol.

4. Try to show an interest in your child's activities. Watch the football game, and go to the drama production or the chorus recital.

5. Activities give children a sense of belonging, which is particularly essential for teenagers.

4

RANDOM THOUGHTS ON PARENTING CHILDREN OF ALL AGES

FRIENDS

1. Even young children need to have play dates to learn how to get along socially.

2. As children grow up, they will sometimes choose friends whom their parents don't approve of for one reason or another. After a certain age, children need to select their own friends. Their parents may not like their selection and may feel that these friends are a bad influence on their child. However, when children become teenagers, the parent's remark "I don't want you to see so and so" is the beginning of trouble. Instantly that criticized friend will become much more important and interesting to your child.

3. If your child has chosen an "undesirable friend," try to make him or her appear unsavory to your child without having to say a word. Invite the friend to visit in your home. Your child will then be able to make comparisons between your family and your values and his new friend. It also offers you the opportunity to supervise and control the situation to be sure that your worst fears aren't realized.

4. It is wise to get other parents of teenagers involved early in the school year. It is very helpful for you and your children's friends' parents to meet and establish a few general rules that everyone agrees to follow. Then your

child can never say "Joe is allowed to stay out until 2:00 a.m." because you and Joe's parents have already established that the curfew agreed upon is midnight. This works like a charm.

CELL PHONES AND ALL ELECTRONIC DEVICES

1. Cell phones are great for emergencies and immediate communication, but they divert our attention too much from the people we are with in the present. Sometimes they cause us to ignore our children. Witness the parents bringing their small children to school. They walk hand in hand to the classroom door while constantly talking on their cell phones.

E-mailing, tweeting, going on Facebook, watching videos, and so on are all time consuming for the young person. More importantly, much of the subject matter of all these devices is, to say the very least, inappropriate.

2. Cell phones are also used to keep children under constant surveillance. Children are required to report often to their parents by phone, or they are called. This is a good plan when judiciously followed. However, it has been documented that children in college are calling home sometimes as often as three times a day.[1] This is excessive and would have been unheard of in the past.

Some students seem unable to make their own decisions and are always calling home to get advice. They are not learning how to cope without family intervention or interference. This intermeshing and dependence upon family members keep students at the center of attention and prevent their using their own space and time to mature.

TV, COMPUTERS, VIDEO GAMES, FACEBOOK, TWEETING, AND THE LIKE

1. A great deal of research now indicates that too much involvement watching television, playing video games, and using a computer can be harmful to children three years of age and younger.[2] This of course is true for middle-schoolers and teens. It is particularly troubling to see four young people

together anywhere and they are all talking on their cell phones or tweeting, et cetera, to people who aren't there. They are not learning to socialize with each other. They are not learning to be social, negotiate problems, or become what is known as "pals or friends."

There is too much information immediately being given out for people, both young and old, to process successfully. This is causing depression, anxiety, and social problems. Our brains need time and space to sort things out. This is being taken away and results in a lot of antisocial behavior.

2. Reliable research also indicates that too much TV watching is harmful for all children. Because the pictures on TV are presented in little visual bytes, the brain becomes used to this rapid-fire exposure. This often causes problems with children's attention in school.

3. TV, video games, and computers should not take the place of make-believe and other games that children create on their own. These devices, however, are tempting to use, as they keep children quietly occupied.[3]

4. Children who spend too much time watching TV, going online, and using cell phones and any other electronic devices often seem to become passive or aggressive and can't seem to amuse themselves by playing or doing things constructively. Creativity is learned by doing. Social skills are learned by being social.

5. It is recommended that watching TV, playing video games, and using a computer should have specific time limits. For example, TV watching might be a one-hour-a-day activity.[4]

SCHEDULES

1. It is hard to maintain simple schedules these days. There are too many choices for children. Try to use restraint when scheduling extracurricular activities.

2. A great deal of research emphasizes how important play is for children. They learn to share, get along with others, create their own games, and simply enjoy free time. Too many of today's activities are structured, and the just-mentioned skills are not being learned. Adults are always present to settle disagreements and tell children what to do.

Who plays on first base is not decided among the children but assigned by a coach. Getting along with others is the most important skill a child can learn. It is difficult to practice this when adults are supervising all of the child's activities.[5]

3. Play dates and time after school to just hang out with one's friends are extremely important for a child's mental health as well as pure enjoyment and relaxation.

4. Participating in one or two extracurricular activities is reasonable for most young children. A child should commit to the activity for a certain period of time. If six lessons have been paid for, the child must complete them. If he doesn't care for the activity after the six lessons, he may discontinue it. Activities must be tried for a while to determine if the child truly enjoys them. Children who are allowed to stop participating whenever they like will find it difficult to learn to persevere in their work when things become challenging.

5. Children don't need to try every sport or musical instrument or art class by the time they are ten years old. Many people learn to play the piano or take up tennis when they are young adults. They may enjoy the activities more and will work on them more diligently than a young child would. Burnout may occur when one begins activities too soon. It is fun to look forward to learning new things at all ages.

HOMEWORK

1. Homework seems to loom as the biggest school issue. I know I am swimming against the current tide; however, I believe that homework is not appropriate until children are at least in the third grade.[6] (Finland is ranked above all other nations as having the best educational system. No homework is assigned to any child below third grade.)

2. Homework should help teachers assess what they have taught. If your child's homework isn't being checked by the teacher, make an appointment with the teacher to find out why.

3. This has been said once but needs saying again. Insist that your child's homework allows for (1) a proper bedtime, (2) a pleasant family mealtime, (3) play dates or hangout time, and (4) extracurricular activities several times

a week. Make an appointment with your child's teacher if you feel there is too much homework. Five parents calling a teacher about this issue sometimes can make her or him see the light.

4. The sooner you are not involved in any way with your child's homework, the better. Provide a reasonably consistent (There's that word again!) time each day for homework and an appropriate work space. Then stay out of the way unless you are asked specifically for help. Sometimes a parent's lengthy explanations only confuse the child rather than help. Your way to do arithmetic may be outdated or different from the teacher's.

OTHER SCHOOL ISSUES

1. If your child seems to be struggling unduly, schedule a conference with the teachers involved and the principal.

2. Perhaps working with a tutor may benefit your child.

3. Sometimes a psycho-educational battery of testing will help to assess a learning interference that may require some intervention. A good psychologist

will give you a complete picture of your child's learning style and will suggest appropriate home and classroom interventions to help your child learn efficiently and comfortably. Strategies and ideas to help your child reach his or her potential should also be addressed. It is important to know a child's academic potential so his or her teachers and parents do not try to push the student beyond his or her ability. This results in frustration for everyone.

4. Some parents place too much emphasis on their desire for their children to be academically brilliant. We are not all gifted in academics. It is important for parents to understand and accept their children's strengths and weaknesses for learning at school and in all their activities. We need to value and accept our children as they are, not as we wish them to be.

PARENTS NEED TIME FOR THEMSELVES

1. Everyone needs time and space for themselves. By the age of three, my children knew I would need a half hour for myself after work for a bubble bath or a cup of tea. After that break I was relaxed and ready to deal with their onslaught of questions or discussions about their activities.

2. It is a basic human need to have a break. Parents need to schedule a date at least once a week so they can go out to dinner by themselves. They also need to take vacations without their children. You can take your children on half of your vacations, but parents need to work and play together by themselves as well. Someday your little ones will be grown and gone from your home. It is impossible to maintain a healthy marriage with little people constantly interrupting every private conversation and moment.

3. Children need to know that there are authority figures other than their parents. Hiring babysitters from time to time provides good role models for children. The children learn to take direction from others. Of course, you must use discretion when selecting babysitters.

4. Children need to be in bed in the evening so couples can remain in touch with one another through conversations that don't include little voices.

5. Adults need time to associate with other adults to discuss topics other than their children. Who is going to solve the problems of the world if the adults focus only on their children?

6. Your children are not your friends until they are older. You need adult friends in the present and in the future when your children have left the nest.

DISCIPLINE

1. *Discipline* according to Merriam Webster refers to the "training" of children to develop their "self-control, character, orderliness and efficiency." This is different from punishment, which implies penalizing a person—in this case a child—who has misbehaved or "done something wrong." Discipline involves correcting and guiding children on a regular, daily basis. Punishment involves administering a penalty for misbehavior. Hopefully it would be used only rarely by parents in dealing with their children.

2. If parents are consistent in enforcing the few, important rules that have been established at home, they shouldn't have to punish their children often.

3. If a child has misbehaved, he or she should experience a logical consequence. If that doesn't work, a penalty or punishment might be administered. The punishment should "fit the crime" whenever possible. For example, if a child scribbles on the living room wall, he must clean it.

4. Consequences should be given at the moment the child has misbehaved if possible. However, if you are in your car and Johnny has hit Mary, the consequences will have to be delayed for safety's sake.

5. Try to be calm and firm but kind and consistent when dealing with your children in both good and stressful situations.

6. If parents condone or ignore their child's misbehavior, this will encourage the behavior, and it will continue.

7. On the other hand, it is important to note that sometimes, when you are with your children, it is helpful to be selectively blind and deaf. Don't see or hear everything they are doing, or you will be in a constant disciplinary mode, which is not fun for anybody. Pick your battles for just the most important issues. Then you will have some impact and can enforce the consequences consistently.

NOTES

1. Megan Gambino, "Technology Keeps Kids Closer to Parents When Away at College," *Addison Independent*, August 17, 2006, 3A.
2. Lindsey Tanner, "Toddlers Watching TV Risk Attention Problems," *Miami Herald*, April 5, 2004, 1A. The article quotes Dr. Dimitri Christakis, researcher at Children's Hospital and Regional Medical Center in Seattle, WA.
3. John Rosemond, "Pull the Plug on Television without Regrets," *Miami Herald*. Rosemond mentions two titles, *The Plug-In Drug* (1977, 1985, 2002) by Marie Winn and *Endangered Minds* (1990, 1999) by Jane M. Healy, for more information on this topic.
4. Janet Stone, "Children Who Stay Glued to TV Miss Out on Key Experiences," *Miami Herald*, November 6, 2004, 3E.
5. Richard Tait, "Let's Play," *Parade Magazine*, July 30, 2006, 6, 7.
6. Nancy Keats, "Schools Turn Down the Heat on Homework," *Wall Street Journal*, January 19, 2007, W1, W12.

PART 1 SUMMARY

Common Sense

1. Where did common sense go? It seems to have disappeared or is at least waning.
2. We don't need to read a dozen different books to answer our questions about children and parenting. Too many opinions can be confusing.
3. Trust your own judgment to do what is best for your children. Believe in yourself and your instincts so that you can make sensible decisions in all situations without constantly relying on the so-called experts.
4. Remember the following key words when dealing with your children: *consistency*, *limits*, *firm but kind*, *consequences*.
5. Relax and enjoy your children. Take breaks for yourself so you will have the energy to enjoy them.

PART 2

LEARNING DISABILITIES

The next section of this booklet is dedicated to one of the most challenging and important jobs of parenting: that of educating your child. You must find the best possible school environment for your child. This means you need to know how your child learns, his or her learning style. You also have to know what to expect of him or her academically so that he or she is challenged but not overwhelmed.

This requires keeping a close eye, knowing the teachers, and also whether there is something, a learning interference, a "disability," that hinders your child from reaching his or her potential.

When my son was in kindergarten, I said to his teacher, "I think Gregory has some learning issues." I was told I was an overanxious mother. By fourth grade Gregory was very skilled in some areas and struggling with others. I was then asked why I hadn't seen this and done something about the discrepancies! As a school psychologist, I have seen many frustrated children, parents, and teachers who cannot understand why a child is not learning when he or she seems to be bright.

This section is an effort to describe learning disabilities in reasonable terms for teachers and parents. The information is presented in one convenient place for easy reference. I also want to point out some current practices that I believe are detrimental to young children.

There have been many books written about learning disabilities, but they require lots of time and energy to read. I have discovered from the distinct perspective of testing for learning disabilities that the terms change on a regular basis. This guide is an effort to demystify these terms.

I do not care for the term *learning disabilities* because it conjures up the idea of sick people. I prefer to use the term *learning interferences*. We all have some stumbling blocks in our learning styles. The important issue is to discover what it is that prevents us from learning efficiently and, therefore, enjoyably. This is usually accomplished through testing. Some of the most useful tests for assessing each learning disability are listed in the pages to follow.

Once a child is aware of what is hindering him or her from achieving, he or she needs to "own" (understand and accept) what the issue or interference is. The next steps are to obtain some intervention that teaches the child skills to help solve the problem or learn to compensate for it. Some suggestions are addressed in this resource.

I also hope to provide parents with information so that, when they approach a teacher or another professional, they will know what questions to ask and will have the vocabulary to discuss their children in terms everyone will understand.

One crucial issue is determining what age is the most appropriate for testing. There are some schools that require intelligence quotient (IQ) testing for three-year-olds. I have a great deal of trouble with this, as children that young are still maturing. The validity and reliability of such testing are questionable.

We seem to be pressuring parents and teachers to teach children at younger and younger ages to do tasks and have skills for which they are not neurologically ready. IQ tests, for example, contain visual and motor tasks that many three- to six-year-olds cannot do. As they mature they can easily accomplish the very same tasks. Have we forgotten Piaget and developmental milestones in our rush to push education and testing at younger and younger age levels?

I am dismayed these days that so many children are being labeled and these labels become self-fulfilling prophecies. We need to use terms to describe each individual child; labels are too limited. It is my hope that more information about learning styles and interferences for parents, teachers, and the children themselves will protect everyone from these pitfalls.

I also want to assure parents who are advised to have a child tested and diagnosed that this is not the end of the world. It is a step on the road to helping a child learn with more ease and feel better about himself or herself. It is hoped that this guide is helpful in relieving parental concern and will actually lead to a positive conclusion.

5

HOW DO YOU RECOGNIZE LEARNING DISABILITIES?

Have you noticed any of the following?

AT SCHOOL

- ☐ Poor basic skills for the child's age and grade level
- ☐ Very little volunteering or participation
- ☐ Poor handwriting, omitting letters and words, poor use of punctuation and capitalization
- ☐ Homework not completed
- ☐ Messy desk and backpack
- ☐ Difficulty with copying from the board or workbook
- ☐ Too many trips to the bathroom
- ☐ Constant movement
- ☐ Impulsivity
- ☐ Immaturity in general for the child's age
- ☐ Unawareness of his or her own space
- ☐ Trouble with time and understanding rhythm
- ☐ Reversing letters and words at the end of first grade or above (It is normal to reverse letters in kindergarten.)
- ☐ Not choosing to do visual tasks when given a choice, such as working on puzzles or building with blocks

- ☐ Not liking listening activities, such as listening to tapes/CDs
- ☐ Difficulty with sequencing, inability to learn such concepts as the days of the week or multiplication tables

AT SCHOOL AND AT HOME

- ☐ Excessive fidgeting
- ☐ Time issues, inability to finish tasks on time, such as dressing or completing chores at home
- ☐ Inability to finish school work or tests in a timely manner
- ☐ Too many questions, inability to understand directions or to follow them
- ☐ Excessive daydreaming
- ☐ Social ineptitude, a lack of friends, isolation
- ☐ Clumsiness, dropping things
- ☐ Poor diction or speaking in a monotone (not to be confused with an accent)
- ☐ Needing too much time to think of an answer (talking around a subject), formulate an idea, or do written work
- ☐ Forced speech
- ☐ Talking loudly, is impolite or confrontational
- ☐ Disliking reading
- ☐ Making excuses

6

TYPES OF LEARNING INTERFERENCES

AUDITORY INTERFERENCES (THE INABILITY TO PROCESS OR UNDERSTAND WHAT ONE HEARS)

The following are the areas in which a child may have difficulty:

- *Auditory discrimination* refers to hearing various sounds and being able to distinguish the differences between them.
- *Auditory memory* involves long- or short-term recall of things one hears.
- *Auditory sequencing and planning* difficulties may be exemplified by a child's inability to learn the multiplication tables or days of the week in order. A child also may be disorganized verbally or seem "spacey" while conversing.
- *Auditory processing* is the ability to understand language and say what one thinks. Auditory processing problems are usually pervasive in all the languages one speaks. For example, in a bilingual person, interferences would be present in both languages.
- *Aphasia* is when the child can hear but is unable to understand what he or she is hearing.
- *Apraxia* is when the child is unable to say what he or she wants to say or what he or she is thinking in a concise manner.
- *Speed* problems occur when the child is unable to function verbally within a reasonable amount of time.

The interferences described in the following four sections are sometimes grouped under the category of nonverbal learning disabilities (NVLD).

VISUAL PERCEPTION AND VISUAL/MOTOR INTERFERENCES

These are sometimes referred to as sensory integration. There are more than eighty places in the brain that help us interpret or perceive what we actually see.

- There is a lack of attention to *visual detail.*
- *Visual memory* is the ability to remember things that one sees or has been shown.
- *Visual closure* is the mind's ability to visualize a whole, such as a number or letter, in its entirety.
- *Visual/spatial relations* involve judging distances and shapes in space.
- *Judging parts-to-whole relationships* is exemplified by the ability to do puzzles or work with fractions.
- *Visual/motor planning* refers to organization skills. It can affect the way a child spaces work on a blank piece of paper. It can also affect the orderliness of a desk or book bag.
- *Visual perception* occurs when the brain interprets objects, drawings, or written material.
- *Visual processing speed* is the ability to work within time limits appropriate for a child's age level.
- *Visual/motor integration* is the ability to perceive and copy material from one place to another.

DYSLEXIA—DIFFICULTY WITH READING OR INTERPRETING THE WRITTEN WORD

- This may be indicated by letter and word reversals, mirror imaging, and/or directional difficulties. These types of reading problems are usually perceptually based.

- Difficulty with reading may also be a phonological problem. A child cannot sound out words easily or hear various sounds.
- Dyslexia also may be caused by language-interpreting difficulties.

MOTOR/SPATIAL-DIRECTIONALITY INTERFERENCES

- *Inability to judge space on a paper* as exemplified by poor spacing and poor handwriting.
- *Inability to judge space involving other people* affects one's social awareness.
- *Directionality* difficulty is exemplified by left and right confusion.
- *Visual/motor integration* or motor problems become evident while writing or copying material from one place to another.

ATTENTION INTERFERENCES

- *Attention deficit disorder (ADD) and attention deficit hyperactivity disorder (ADHD)* are terms that have become popular in the last ten years. In fact I believe too many children obtain this label even at the young age of three or four.
- It has been my discovery attention problems mask many other real learning problems. Many children I have met are often very bright and are therefore curious and busy. They sometimes ask too many questions or poke around a classroom and therefore receive one of two labels—ADD or ADHD.
- Children who have visual motor problems or have trouble with one particular subject and therefore don't stick to the lesson at hand are often seen as "attention" problems. If they are identified with a specific learning interference, that can be accommodated.
- Too many children once labeled ADD or ADHD are placed on medication: Adderall or Ritalin. To my knowledge not a lot of research has been done on the after-effects of these medications on younger children once they have reached older years.
- I have read in more than one source that studies have been done that indicate that neither of these drugs boost children's grades. A study in

Quebec of four thousand children indicated that boys who took one of these drugs actually performed worse in school than those not on the drugs. Girls were reported to have more emotional problems according to a working paper published by the National Bureau of Economic Research, a nonprofit economics research firm.

- In general there isn't much evidence that any of these drugs improve academic progress. The drugs can control focus and self-control, but actual grades do not seem to improve. Lately there have been studies showing that exercise, sleep, and diet can be incredibly influential in helping attention difficulties.
- It is not in many children's best interest to be placed on medication. Many times more testing will indicate why the child is not focusing. It is particularly discouraging to see very young children on these medications, as they have not reached their full mental capacity or physical development. Children normally complete this process between the ages of seven and ten years old. There are "late bloomers" who simply develop normally but more slowly.
- There is some thought that taking these drugs increases other drug dependencies in teenagers and adults. Perhaps we should teach coping skills rather than prescribing pills. Teachers can help in this by providing interesting and varied curriculums that allow children to use their personal skills.

SPEECH AND LANGUAGE INTERFERENCES

- Children may have trouble with articulation and the appropriate pronunciation of words.
- It is difficult for some children to learn any language. This includes their native language as well as others.
- These interferences may sometimes be related to visual or auditory deficits.

EMOTIONAL INTERFERENCES

- Situations at home that cause confusion and affect children include divorce, a relative moving into or out of the home, the death of a pet, or the birth of a sibling.
- There is a lack of self-confidence.
- Emotional interferences are sometimes caused by a child's inability to achieve at school. A bright child who knows he or she is intelligent sometimes cannot do some specific tasks easily. This causes him or her to become angry and frustrated.

- Emotional interferences may be due to inappropriate parenting. Parents may nag, be too critical, or demand perfection.
- There is no discipline at home.
- Children do not learn to be responsible if they are not asked to be.
- Parenting styles may differ, which confuses children.
- When parents do not live together, children have two separate households with which to cope.
- Some children have no responsibilities at home except for their homework.
- Psychological disorders and/or anxiety may cause emotional interferences.

7

WHAT TESTS ASSESS LEARNING INTERFERENCES?

TESTS FOR AUDITORY INTERFERENCES

- Intelligence Quotient (IQ) Testing

  Wechsler Intelligence Scale for Children, Third and Fourth Editions (WISC III and WISC IV)
  Wechsler Preschool and Primary Scale of Intelligence, Fourth Edition (WPPSI-IV)
  Standford Binet Intelligence Test
  Wechsler Adult Intelligence Scale, Third Edition (WAIS III)

- Woodcock Johnson III Tests of Cognitive Abilities: Measures how the brain receives information
- Wepman Test of Auditory Discrimination
- Listening comprehension on the Peabody Individual Achievement Test, Revised; Wechsler Individual Achievement Test, Revised; and Woodcock Johnson III Tests of Achievement
- Achievement Tests: Dictated math on the Wechsler, Woodcock, and Peabody

  Key Math includes only computational problems.
  Listening is not involved.

- Gray Oral Reading Test, Third Edition: A timed reading test
- Anecdotal: Repeating information

TESTS FOR VISUAL AND PERCEPTUAL INTERFERENCES

- Wechsler Intelligence Scale for Children, Third and Fourth Editions
- Writing Sample
- Woodcock Johnson III: Achievement and cognitive tests
- Bender Gestalt: Reproduce designs
- Beery-Buktenica Developmental Test of Visual/Motor Integration, Fifth Edition
- Drawings
- Puzzle/Mazes: Actually doing them with the tester
- Test of Nonverbal Intelligence, Third Edition (TONI 3)

TESTS FOR MOTOR OR SPATIAL INTERFERENCES

- Beery-Buktenica Developmental Test of Visual/Motor Integration, Fifth Edition
- Bender Gestalt
- Drawings
- Writing Sample
- Quick Neurological Screening Test, Revised Edition

TESTS FOR ATTENTION DEFICIT

- Stroop Color and Word Test
- Gordon Diagnostic System: A computer test
- Wisconsin Card Sorting Test
- Parents' and teachers' rating scales: Subjective (for example, the Conners)
- Anecdotal

TESTS FOR EMOTIONAL INTERFERENCES

- Bender Gestalt
- Drawings

- Rotter Sentence Completion for Children
- Thematic Apperception Test (TAT)
- Roberts Apperception Test for Children
- Minnesota Multiphasic Personality Inventory 2
- Rorschach
- Self-reports

There are newer tests or other tests that are used, but I personally feel very comfortable to this day using the tests mentioned in this chapter.

8

SUGGESTED STRATEGIES FOR TEACHERS

1. Recommend a tutor who will not just help with homework but will also teach the child skills to surmount the difficulty. Do not expect the child to catch up immediately. Obtain books and materials from the previous grade level so that the child can master them easily and enjoy learning.

- Ask the parents to do some drills at home, such as multiplication tables, vocabulary, and so on. These should be enjoyable activities and should not lead to confrontation between parent and child.
- Find out why the child is behind: new at school, new to the United States?
- Love of learning is the main goal. Frustration diminishes this and lowers self-esteem.

2. Fidgeting may be a symptom of anxiety or a lack of ability to attend or focus.

- Allow the child to work for a short period of time; provide breaks.
- Allow the child to exercise at recess and during class at various times. Do not withhold recess as a punishment for not completing tasks. All children need breaks during the school day.

3. Give extra time to children who need it. Modify their assignments or the number of problems required.

- For example, a child could be asked to complete just the even-numbered math problems.
- Many children with *visual/motor* difficulties have trouble copying assignments from the blackboard or whiteboard. Their homework assignments could be provided in writing by the teacher. Computers can be a big help to a child with this type of learning interference.

4. If a child is unable to understand directions presented orally, he or she should be given them in writing. Read directions aloud slowly and repeat them. Watch the children's faces to be sure they understand.

5. Find out why a child is not volunteering. Call on the child in a gentle manner. Go around the room so the child has time to figure out the answer before it is his or her turn. This will help the child to avoid embarrassment.

6. Poor handwriting and omissions of letters, words, or numbers may indicate visual difficulties. The child may need extra time.

- Use lined paper for written work. Children may benefit by using computers.
- For children with *fine motor* problems, assign less writing with emphasis on quality rather than quantity.
- Cover parts of his or her paper so the child can focus on one word or math problem at a time.
- Stress accurate proofreading; children can exchange papers and proofread for one another on some assignments. Some children will never be good proofreaders.

7. Try to determine why a child is daydreaming.

- Does he or she seem not to be listening yet understands the information he or she is hearing? Have the child sit at the front of the class and tap on his or her desk occasionally to bring him back to task rather than saying his or her name repeatedly.

8. To help children learn social skills, have them team up in pairs or groups to learn or work on projects.

- Talk to parents about play dates.
- Talk about social skills in class, discussing how to make and be friends. Make this part of a writing assignment or actually role-play social situations.

9. Try to help clumsy, disorganized children by assisting them in keeping their desks in order.

- Another child might be assigned to help them with this as a buddy to prevent embarrassment.
- Notes could be placed in backpacks to be sure they are taken home.

10. If a child's homework is not completed, communicate with parents to find out why.

- The child might lose some privileges at home if homework is repeatedly not done. Taking away recess and/or PE class is counterproductive.
- Have a conference with parents to find out how much time a child is spending on homework.
- A timer might be suggested with instructions about using it effectively.
- Make a chart to reward the child when homework is completed.
- Communicate with parents so they can reinforce the teacher's efforts at home.

11. If a child has messy habits, ask parents to help with the backpack assembly at home. A classmate might help at school.

- Some children are unable to organize well. This is an intrinsic problem that may need special attention.
- Many bright people are disorganized.

12. Recommend a speech evaluation if a child needs it.

- Encourage children to speak slowly, and give them adequate time.
- Some children are reticent to speak in front of others.

13. For visual/motor integration issues, one can suggest doing puzzles, dot-to-dot pictures, and mazes.

- Tracing numbers, letters, and words will also be helpful.
- Give the child a copy of his or her homework assignments in writing. Then he or she will have a copy of what is written on the blackboard.

14. For directionality issues use a star or other picture at the top left corner of the child's paper to show where to start writing. Arrows might be used to indicate directionality.

15. Do not pressure children who have trouble expressing themselves orally. Anxiety makes the problem worse.

- A language evaluation should be recommended. Give the child some practice in making concise statements.
- Start with questions that can be easily answered.
- Discuss the main idea in paragraphs and the meaning of new vocabulary words.

16. A child may be overanxious and want to avoid being in class.

- Sometimes children ask to use the bathroom too frequently. Find out if this is a physical problem.
- Talk with the child. Recommend that the child's parents discuss this with their pediatrician.

17. Forced speech may indicate anxiety, so talk with the parents.

- Speech therapy may be warranted.

18. Constant movement may stem from anxiety or a physical inability to sit still.

- Ignore this whenever possible if the child is learning and not disturbing others in class.
- The younger the child, the more stretching, movement, and recesses he or she needs.
- It is recognized that some children learn better when they are moving some part of their bodies or even when standing up.

19. When dealing with acting-out behavior, one must find out when and why it is occurring.

- These behaviors may indicate anger, or a possible hearing or social learning problem.
- Talk with the child quietly by himself or herself to see if there is a problem at home. A bright child with small motor or perceptual problems may become frustrated. He or she knows he or she is smart but cannot perform some tasks as well or as easily as classmates. This results in acting-out behavior.
- Talk with parents to see if you can discover what is frustrating or bothering the child.

20. If a child dislikes reading, have his or her reading comprehension level assessed.

- Obtain books for the child at an earlier grade level. High Noon Books have a high-interest, low-vocabulary level.
- It is important for children to be encouraged to love reading.
- Work on increasing vocabulary.
- Parents can develop games at home to encourage their children to learn new words every day.

21. Impulsive children need to be encouraged to take another look and slow down.

- Put a quotation on their desks: "Have you thought about this?"
- Try to determine why they want to do things so quickly.

22. If a child's physical development seems slow, he or she needs to be given the gift of time.

- Try to establish if his or her parents are treating the child at the appropriate age level or if they are babying him or her. Children behave in the manner and at the age level at which they are treated.
- There is often a dichotomy when parents baby a child but expect him or her to act maturely in school. This is confusing to the child.

23. Try not to accept excuses.

- Question the child.
- Communicate with parents to determine why things are not being accomplished.

24. Children who have trouble with understanding space may need some help.

- They may stand too close to peers and annoy them.
- Occupational or physical therapy may help them with this issue.

25. With a more varied, interesting, and well-timed school day comes an improved learning atmosphere. Ask children to do actual physical projects, artwork, or even drama productions. All these spark interest and appeal to various styles of learning. Some children learn by listening, others by seeing, and still others with hands-on activities.

9

SUGGESTED STRATEGIES FOR PARENTS

1. Read aloud to one another. This is good for everyone!

    - Select stories that have easy vocabulary familiar to the child. This should be fun and not a struggle.

2. Communicate with teachers.

    - Cultivate an open and friendly relationship.
    - Take teachers seriously.

3. If a child is struggling, be willing to seek help.

    - Testing
    - Tutoring
    - Therapy

4. After testing, ask for specific suggestions you can try at home.

    - Read to and with your child (aloud and silently). Take turns reading one paragraph at a time.
    - If it causes friction when the parent helps the child with homework, consider hiring a homework coach.

- Put vocabulary words on the refrigerator. Use positive rewards to encourage the child to memorize them by the end of the week.
- For children with visual/motor difficulties, do dot-to-dot pictures, mazes, and puzzles and trace letters, numbers, and words.
- Hire a tutor trained to understand your child's learning interference.

5. Plan productive activities to keep children busy. Computer games and TV are passive and in general do not stimulate one's imagination.

6. Establish a quiet place to do homework.

- Keep other siblings from disturbing the child.
- Reduce all distractions, including ringing telephones.
- Use a timer to help children stick to the task. Set the timer for the amount of time the child thinks he or she will need. See if the child achieves the prediction. The child will become engaged in this "beat the clock" game.

7. Treat children in a calm, businesslike, but kind manner. Be positive and patient.

8. Give instructions in a brief, concise manner.

- Start with one command at a time and gradually increase the number. This should be age appropriate.
- Older children should be able to handle more than three instructions unless they have a learning interference.
- Make sure you have the child's attention before giving directions.
- Post rules or chores in a conspicuous place, such as the refrigerator door.
- Try to differentiate between hyperactive, uncontrollable behavior and simple, typical misbehavior.

9. All children need adequate sleep (ten to twelve hours per night). Children with learning issues work harder in school and often require more rest than others.

10. Have hanging-out or free time for children every day, if possible. Children need time to chase mental rainbows or lie on their backs and watch clouds.

11. Exercise is essential to healthy bodies and minds. Breaks from school-related work with time to move around have been documented to increase children's learning power and memory.

12. Help disorganized children with their backpacks every evening before bed to relieve the morning's scurry. Clothes also may be selected at night for the next day.

13. Structure in a daily schedule, such as regular bedtimes and mealtimes, helps all children, particularly those who tend to be disorganized. Organizing rooms where things are easy to find is also helpful.

14. Teach children self-assertive behavior; children with learning interferences may be overlooked. Their individual needs may be missed by adults working with them.

- Let the child know that it is all right to ask for help.
- Inform the child that the world's smartest people ask questions.

15. Access to a computer by third grade is important for children with visual/perceptual or visual/motor problems.

16. Provide children who find school difficult with such activities as sports, dance classes, music, art, or karate. Choose activities in which they can be successful so they will gain self-respect and self-confidence.

17. Limit TV and video games as well as too much cell phone use, screen time, and so on. Parents should be careful to monitor cell phone conversations and online activity, like tweeting. They should also warn their children about the lack of privacy on Facebook and the like. Research suggests that too much passive TV watching, using computers, and playing video games may damage the intellectual abilities of children under the age of four. For older children, too much involvement in these activities may be addictive.

18. Encourage healthy eating. Too much emphasis on eating habits and clean plates may cause problems later.

19. Teach children "self-talk" skills, problem-solving techniques, and visualization skills.

20. Be aware of your child's friendships to ensure a positive social life. Play dates may be hard to establish, but they are essential to healthy development.

21. Use natural consequences as much as possible to discipline children. For example, not studying may lead to failure on a test.

22. You can help children to strengthen their auditory skills by listening to audio tapes in the car or at home.

23. Rhythm and music can facilitate learning for some children. Singing the times tables or dancing while reciting a poem sometimes helps with retention.

24. If your child is having trouble with friendships, have him or her tested for a social interference. Some children do not read social clues naturally. They misinterpret facial expressions and body language. They need to be taught social skills. There are classes given by language pathologists called pragmatics; some psychologists conduct social skills groups.

25. Reversals in letters and numbers before and including most of first grade may be part of a child's normal development. Children continue to develop until they are eight years old. Beyond that age reversals may indicate a true interference. There are some children who are "late bloomers."

- Having the child trace numbers and letters while looking at and saying them (using a multimodal system of seeing, hearing, and touching) is helpful.
- Older children may be taught intellectual strategies to help them correct the positions of letters and numbers. For example, in the word *bed*, note the direction of *b* and *d*.

26. Encourage auditory activities.

- Use games, videotapes, DVDs, CDs, or MP3s.
- Read aloud to children. This may help to develop their auditory skills.

27. An inability to sequence is a common but little-diagnosed learning interference. Sometimes music may be helpful; the child may sing the multiplication tables, dance, or move his or her hands while singing them.

28. It is helpful for children to have their interferences identified for them. Understanding the problem will lower their frustration level.

29. Analog watches are recommended for children. It helps them "see" the passage of time, which is good for slow or rapid processors.

10

WHAT IF YOUR CHILD'S SCHOOL PROFESSIONALS OR PEDIATRICIAN RECOMMEND A PSYCHO-EDUCATIONAL BATTERY OF TESTING?

Such a battery may include intelligence, achievement, processing, and psychological tests. Interview several clinical or school psychologists.

- Ask them for their opinions or philosophies about education, maturation issues, and medication.
- Ask about the time frame for their reports.

Batteries of tests differ among professionals.

- Determine what needs to be addressed.
- Be certain that the tester includes the necessary tests. For example, if there are possible emotional/social issues, the battery should include psychological tests called projective tests.

Be sure you will have a chance to meet the tester after the testing for a thorough discussion of the results, including explanations and recommendations.

Prepare your child for the actual experience. The tester can suggest what to say to the child before testing. Most children love the whole process. It should be enjoyable. The child receives the tester's undivided attention without interruption.

- Most children enjoy learning about themselves if the testing is done in a friendly and relaxed manner.

After the testing, several interventions might be recommended:

Tutoring may help the child catch up or learn strategies to compensate for his or her learning interference. The latter often requires a specialist trained in working with children with learning interferences.

Therapy may help the child:

- Cope with understanding his or her learning style
- Deal with family issues
- Address inappropriate behaviors
- Learn socialization skills

Occupational and physical therapy:

- May be recommended for children with fine and gross motor issues or visual/perceptual problems
- May also be helpful for children with spatial and directional problems

Placement in specific educational environments designed for students with special needs may also be helpful.

PART 2 SUMMARY

It is most helpful after a learning interference has been identified to help the child learn to "own his or her problem." Understanding what is "wrong" with his or her learning style will lower the child's frustration level.

- When teachers and parents have been informed that a child has a learning interference, they will generally give the child some sympathy and understanding. The child will know that they are aware that some tasks are more difficult because of his or her interference.
- The child will then begin to accept his or her difference and learn to compensate for it.

A learning disability never should be allowed to be used as a crutch or an excuse.

For most learning interferences, a multimodal system of teaching that simultaneously utilizes the child's hearing, seeing, and touching is appropriate. For example, in learning the word *was*, the child would say it aloud letter by letter while tracing the letters with his or her finger.

Tap into, encourage, and help to develop your child's natural talents and instincts.

Learning disabilities or interferences remain the same over time. The names change as people give them new titles. This is like "reinventing the wheel."

Everyone is "wired" differently. We need to tolerate these differences and be aware of them when educating our children.

Education should be about teaching children to love learning and to know how to find the information they seek. It seems that teaching and learning have not improved with the emphasis on more and sooner.

OTHER RESOURCES

Armstrong, Thomas. *The Myth of the A.D.D. Child: 50 Ways to Improve Your Child's Behavior and Attention Span without Drugs, Labels, or Coercion.* New York: Dutton, 1995.

Crook, William G. *Help for the Hyperactive Child: A Good-Sense Guide for Parents of Children with Hyperactivity, Attention Deficits, and Other Behavior and Learning Problems.* Jackson, TN: Professional Books, 1991.

Hallowell, Edward M., and John J. Ratey. *Driven to Distraction: Recognizing and Coping with Attention Deficit Disorder from Childhood through Adulthood.* New York: Anchor Books, 2011.

Levine, Melvin D. *Keeping a Head in School: A Student's Book about Learning Abilities and Learning Disorders.* Cambridge, MA: Educators Publishing Service, 1990.

———. *A Mind at a Time.* New York: Simon and Schuster, 2002.

Olivier, Carolyn, and Rosemary F. Bowler. *Learning to Learn.* New York: Simon and Schuster, 1996.

Osman, Betty B. *Learning Disabilities: A Family Affair.* New York: Warner Books, 1980.

———. *No One to Play With—The Social Side of Learning Disabilities.* New York: Random House, 1982.

Phelan, Thomas W. *1-2-3 Magic: Effective Discipline for Children 2–12.* 4th ed. Glen Ellyn, IL: 2010.

Reichenberg-Ullman, Judyth, and Robert Ullman. *Ritalin-Free Kids: Safe and Effective Homeopathic Medicine for ADHD and Other Behavioral and Learning Problems.* 3rd ed. Edmonds, WA: Picnic Point Press, 2012.

Rosemond, John K. *The New Six-Point Plan for Raising Happy, Healthy Children.* Kansas City, MO: Andrews McMeel, 2006.

Stevens, Suzanne H. *The Learning-Disabled Child: Ways That Parents Can Help.* Winston-Salem, NC: J. F. Blair, 1980.

Wood, Chip. *Yardsticks: Children in the Classroom, Ages 4–14.* 3rd ed. Turners Falls, MA: Northeast Foundation for Children, 2007.

WEBSITES

www.schwablearning.org
LD Online, www.ldonline.org
LD Resources, www.ldresources.com
Learning Disabilities of America, www.ldam.org

ABOUT THE AUTHOR

Susan Maynard is a licensed school psychologist and has been a marriage and family therapist. She has been in private practice for thirty years and has been a consultant to schools in Miami-Dade County. Dr. Maynard is an expert in psycho-educational testing. She helps to identify and treat children with learning interferences and behavior problems. She works with parents to help them understand these interferences and obtain interventions for their children. She can be contacted at tizsusan@gmail.com.